Perfect PENALTY KICK!

The U.S. Women's Soccer Team at the 1999 World Cup

By James Buckley Jr.
Illustrated by Tom Rogers

BEARPORT
PUBLISHING

Minneapolis, Minnesota

BEAR CLAW

Credits

Cover art by Tom Rogers. Photos: 20: © Leonard Zhukovsky/Shutterstock; 21 top: © PA Wire/Newscom; 21 bottom © Erik McGregor/SIPA USA/Newscom; 22 © Feelphoto/Shutterstock; 23 © StefG/Dreamstime.

Bearport Publishing Company Product Development Team
President: Jen Jenson; Director of Product Development: Spencer Brinker; Managing Editor: Allison Juda; Associate Editor: Naomi Reich; Senior Designer: Colin O'Dea; Associate Designer: Elena Klinkner; Associate Designer: Kayla Eggert; Product Development Specialist: Anita Stasson

Produced by Shoreline Publishing Group LLC
Santa Barbara, California
Designer: Patty Kelley
Editorial Director: James Buckley Jr.

DISCLAIMER: This graphic story is a dramatization based on true events. It is intended to give the reader a sense of the narrative rather than a presentation of actual details as they occurred.

Library of Congress Cataloging-in-Publication Data

Names: Buckley, James, Jr., 1963- author. | Rogers, Tom (Illustrator) illustrator.
Title: Perfect penalty kick! : the U.S. Women's Soccer Team at the 1999 World Cup / by James Buckley Jr. ; illustrated by Tom Rogers.
Description: Minneapolis, MN : Bearport Publishing Company, [2024] | Series: Amazing moments in sports | Includes bibliographical references and index.
Identifiers: LCCN 2023005614 (print) | LCCN 2023005615 (ebook) | ISBN 9798885099936 (library binding) | ISBN 9798888221754 (paperback) | ISBN 9798888223086 (ebook)
Subjects: LCSH: U.S. Women's National Soccer Team--Comic books, strips, etc. | FIFA Women's World Cup (1991 : United States)--Comic books, strips, etc. | LCGFT: Graphic novels. | Nonfiction comics.
Classification: LCC GV944.U5 B83 2024 (print) | LCC GV944.U5 (ebook) | DDC 796.3340973--dc23/eng/20230216
LC record available at https://lccn.loc.gov/2023005614
LC ebook record available at https://lccn.loc.gov/2023005615

For more information, write to Bearport Publishing, 5357 Penn Avenue South, Minneapolis, MN 55419.

CONTENTS

Chapter 1
SOCCER COMES TO AMERICA

JULY 10, 1999
PASADENA,
CALIFORNIA

More than 90,000 people packed the Rose Bowl, while 40 million viewers across the United States tuned in on TV.

SCOREBOARD
USA   CHINA
0   0

The sold-out stadium was buzzing with energy as history unfolded during the 1999 Women's World Cup final between the United States and China.

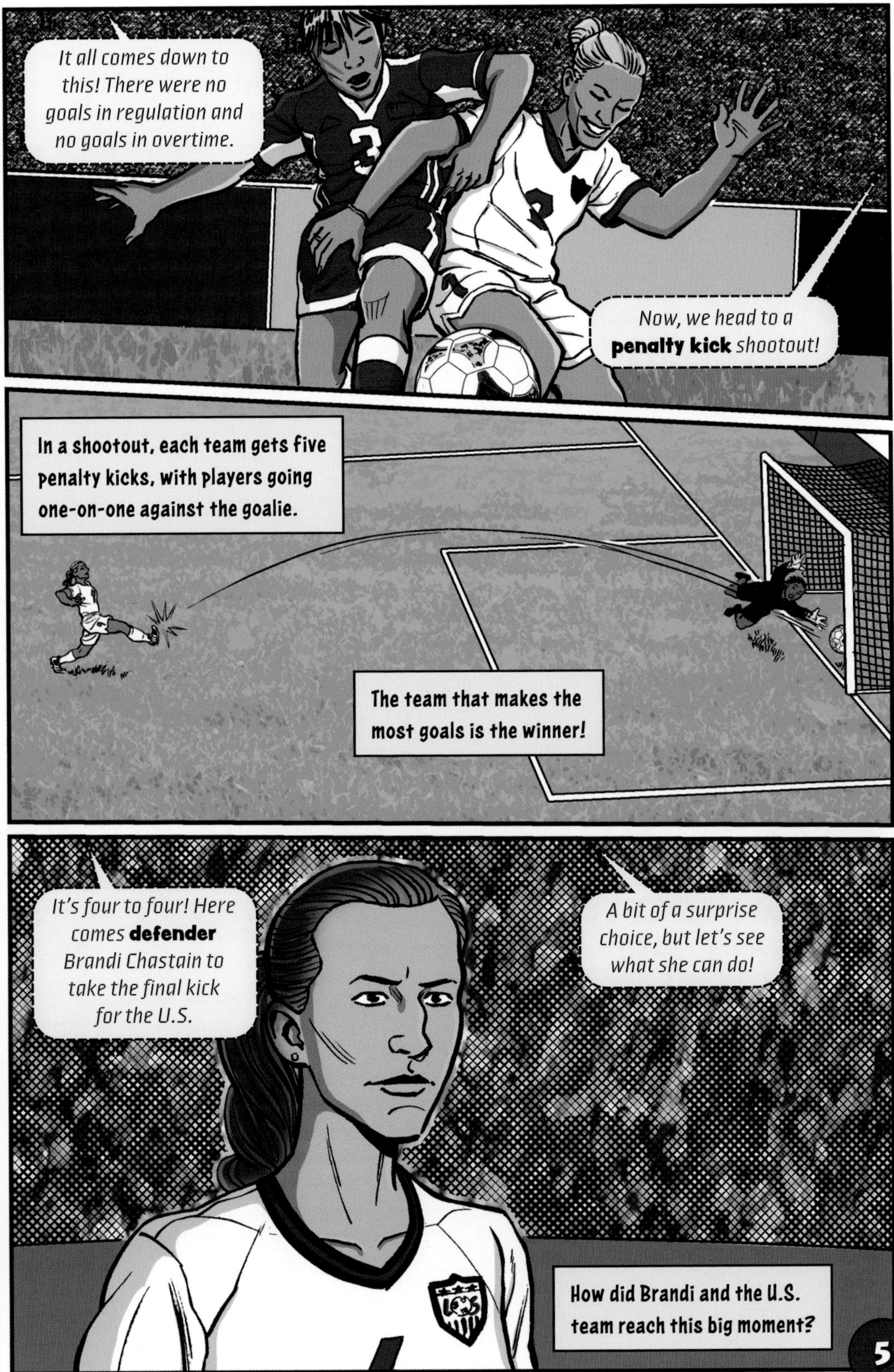
It all comes down to this! There were no goals in regulation and no goals in overtime.
Now, we head to a **penalty kick** shootout!
In a shootout, each team gets five penalty kicks, with players going one-on-one against the goalie.
The team that makes the most goals is the winner!
It's four to four! Here comes **defender** Brandi Chastain to take the final kick for the U.S.
A bit of a surprise choice, but let's see what she can do!
How did Brandi and the U.S. team reach this big moment?

During the early 1990s, soccer wasn't very popular in the United States.

There were only a few **professional** female players, and they made very little money, especially compared to female stars in other sports.

Then in 1994, the men's World Cup was held in America. To everyone's surprise, the tournament was a huge hit.

Fans from around the world packed into sold-out stadiums to watch as Brazil won the championship.

Suddenly, soccer's popularity in the United States skyrocketed.

The **international** soccer community took notice.

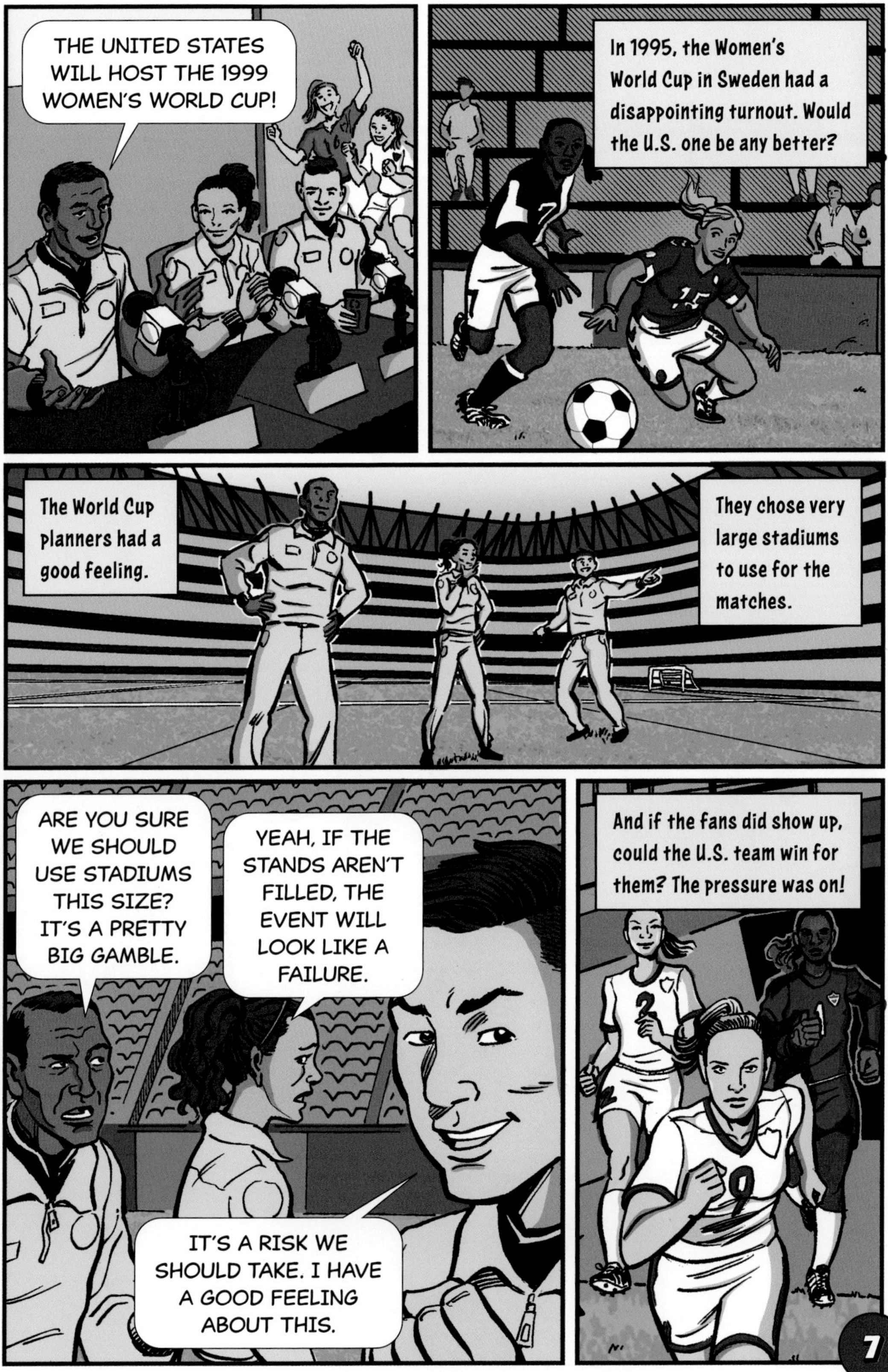

THE UNITED STATES WILL HOST THE 1999 WOMEN'S WORLD CUP!
In 1995, the Women's World Cup in Sweden had a disappointing turnout. Would the U.S. one be any better?
The World Cup planners had a good feeling.
They chose very large stadiums to use for the matches.
ARE YOU SURE WE SHOULD USE STADIUMS THIS SIZE? IT'S A PRETTY BIG GAMBLE.
YEAH, IF THE STANDS AREN'T FILLED, THE EVENT WILL LOOK LIKE A FAILURE.
IT'S A RISK WE SHOULD TAKE. I HAVE A GOOD FEELING ABOUT THIS.
And if the fans did show up, could the U.S. team win for them? The pressure was on!

Chapter 2

THE WORLD CUP

The tournament began with a colorful Opening Ceremony at Giants Stadium in New Jersey.

From the start, it was clear that fans would, indeed, fill the big stadiums.

And the U.S. team didn't disappoint, either. It easily won its three first-round games.

U.S. 3–DENMARK 0

U.S. 7–NIGERIA 1

U.S. 3–NORTH KOREA 0

Next up was the **knock-out** playoffs.

We have exciting **quarterfinal** action here.

Germany is giving the U.S. all it can handle!

Chastain scores! The U.S. has tied the game!

After beating Germany 3-2, the U.S. is shutting out mighty Brazil in this **semifinal**!

Cindy Parlow **heads** in a goal! The U.S. takes the lead!

It's over! The U.S. beats Brazil 2-0!

Next stop—the championship game against China!

We're just about ready to start the World Cup final, and the stadium is packed!

This is believed to be the largest crowd ever to see a women's sports event!

USA! USA!

We Love You!

Both teams are already playing well.

There's a great **tackle** by Chastain! The U.S. defense is staying strong!

But Hamm's shot is blocked by China's goalie Gao Hong!

As the second half began, the score was tied at 0-0. Players from both teams were hot and tired.

What a game! Neither team is giving an inch in this battle!

After 90 minutes, the game remained scoreless. The teams entered 30 minutes of **extra time**. The first team to score would win!

There's a shot... it's past Scurry! But Lilly is there to knock it away!

FWEET!

And that's the end of extra time!

We're going to penalty kicks to decide the champ!

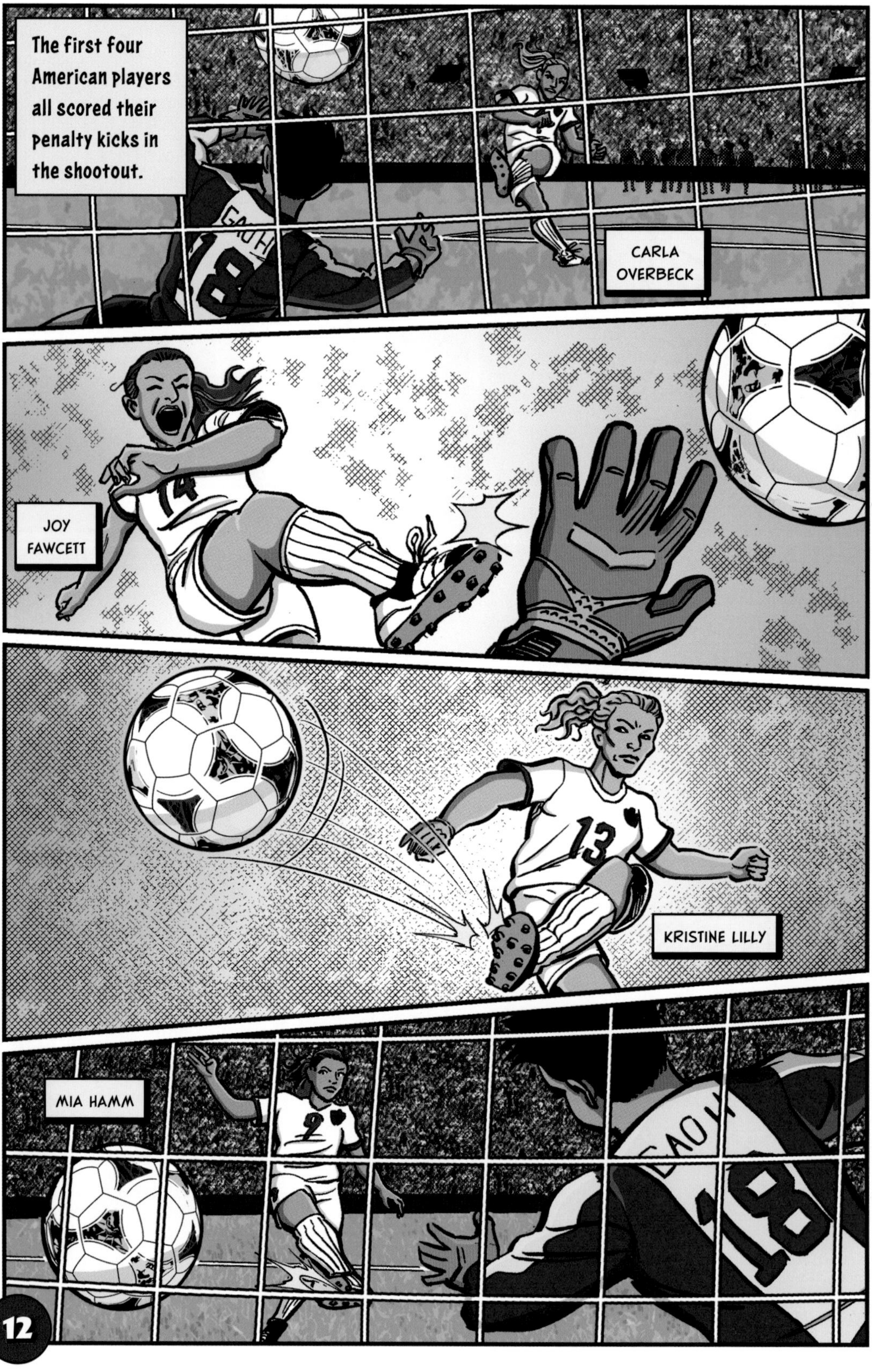
The first four American players all scored their penalty kicks in the shootout.
CARLA OVERBECK
JOY FAWCETT
KRISTINE LILLY
MIA HAMM

Meanwhile, China's players made four of their five penalty kicks.

XIE HUILIN

QIU HAIYAN

ZHAN OUYING

SUN WEN

But there was one very important miss.

Brianna Scurry blocks Liu Ying's penalty kick! She makes the save!

Chapter 3

THE PERFECT KICK

This is the U.S. team's chance for a win. It's all up to Brandi Chastain!

If she makes this kick, her team will be the victors!

A lot was going through Brandi's head.

I'M GLAD THE COACH PICKED ME... BUT I MISSED A PENALTY KICK AGAINST CHINA EARLIER THIS YEAR!

I KNOW! I'LL USE MY LEFT FOOT INSTEAD. SHE MIGHT NOT BE EXPECTING THAT!

Fans in the stands and watching at home were pulling for Brandi!

GO, BRANDI, GO!

I'M SO NERVOUS!

CAN SHE MAKE IT?

YOU CAN DO IT, BRANDI!

KNOCK IT IN!

Brandi knew what she had to do.

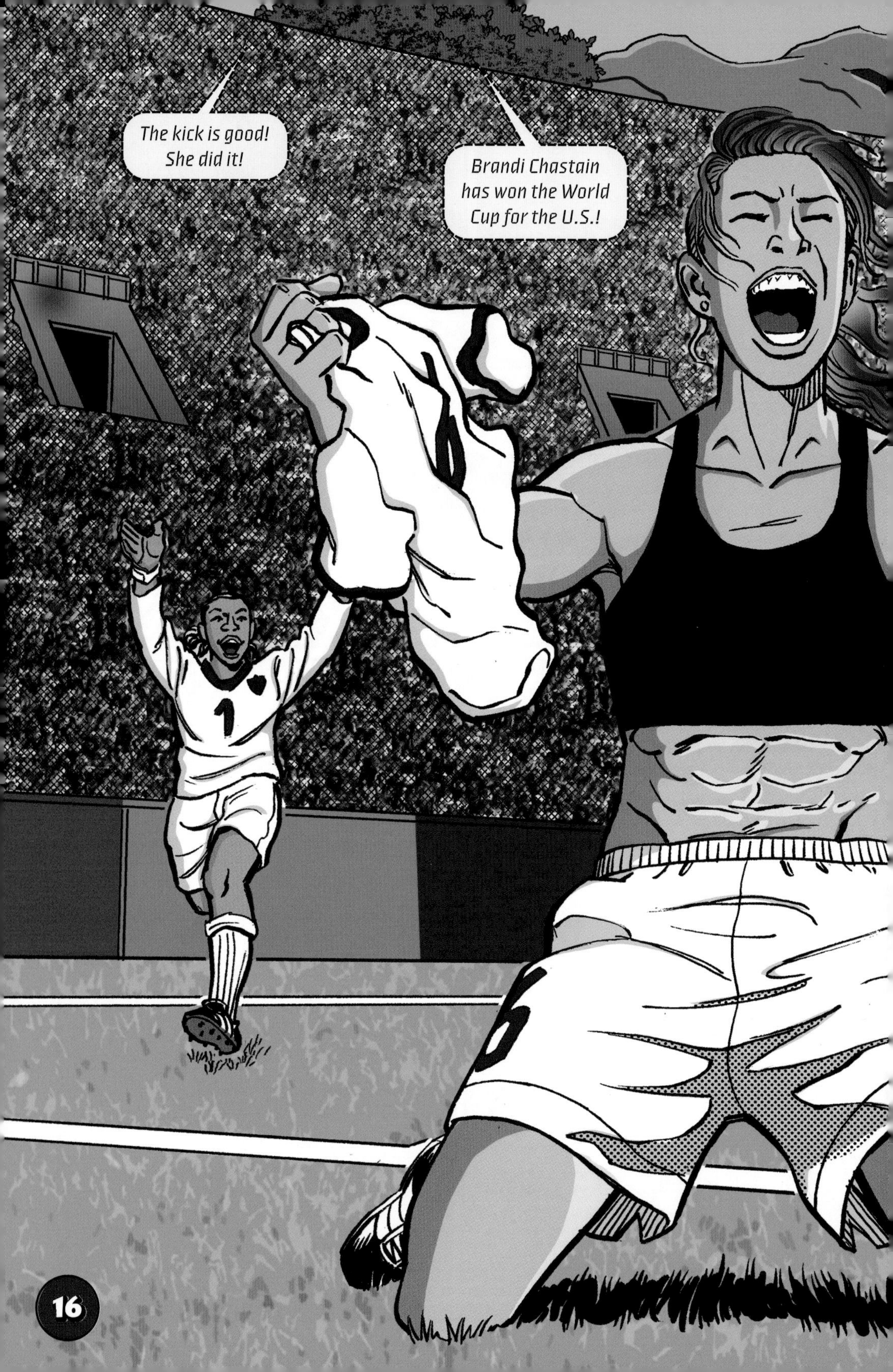
The kick is good! She did it!
Brandi Chastain has won the World Cup for the U.S.!

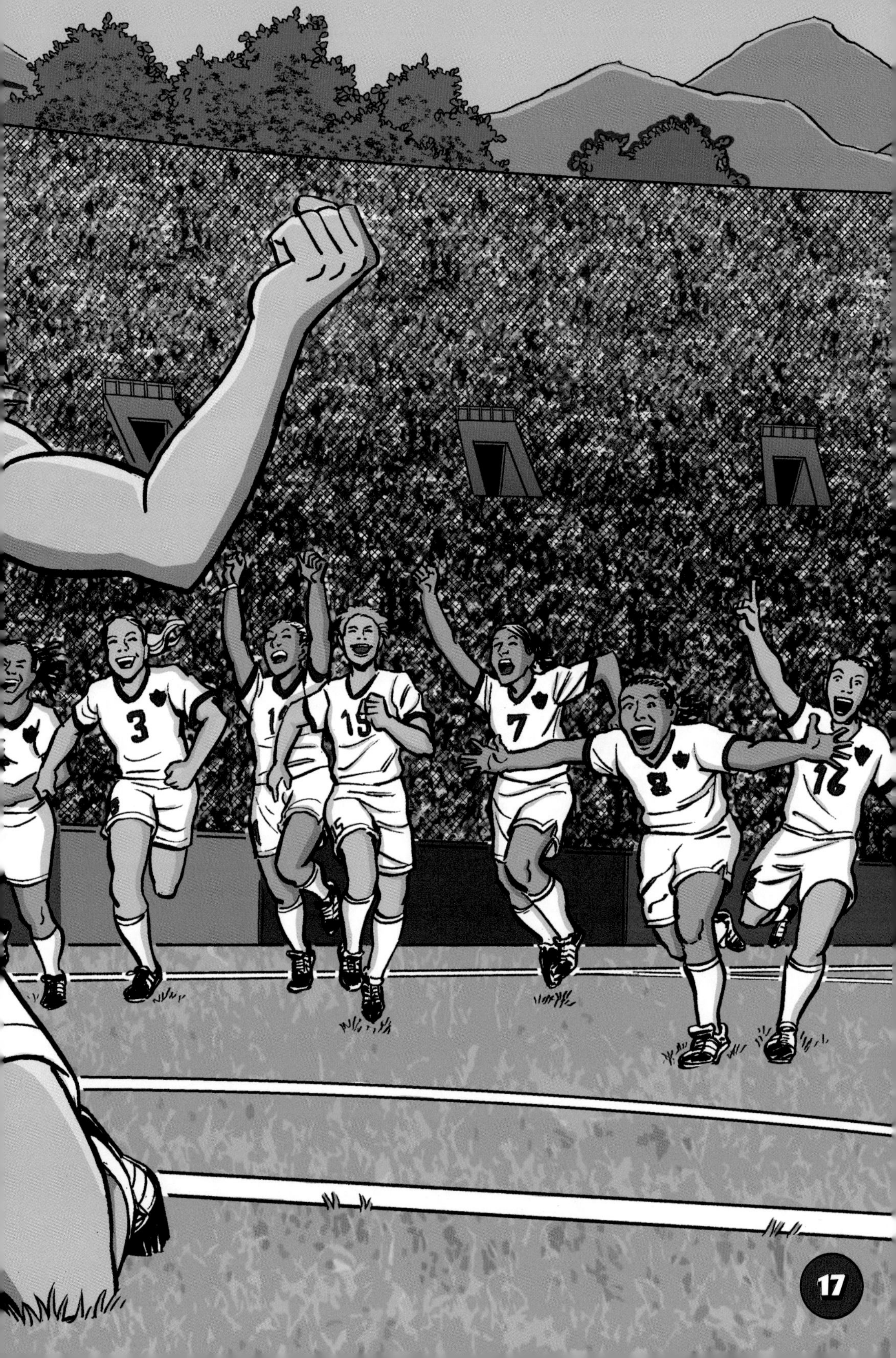

WE DID IT!

As the team celebrated, the 90,000 fans in the stands went wild!

USA! USA! USA!

Team captain Carla Overbeck accepted the World Cup trophy. The whole event had been a huge success.

More than a million people watched the games in person, and tens of millions more watched on TV. Women's soccer had arrived in America!

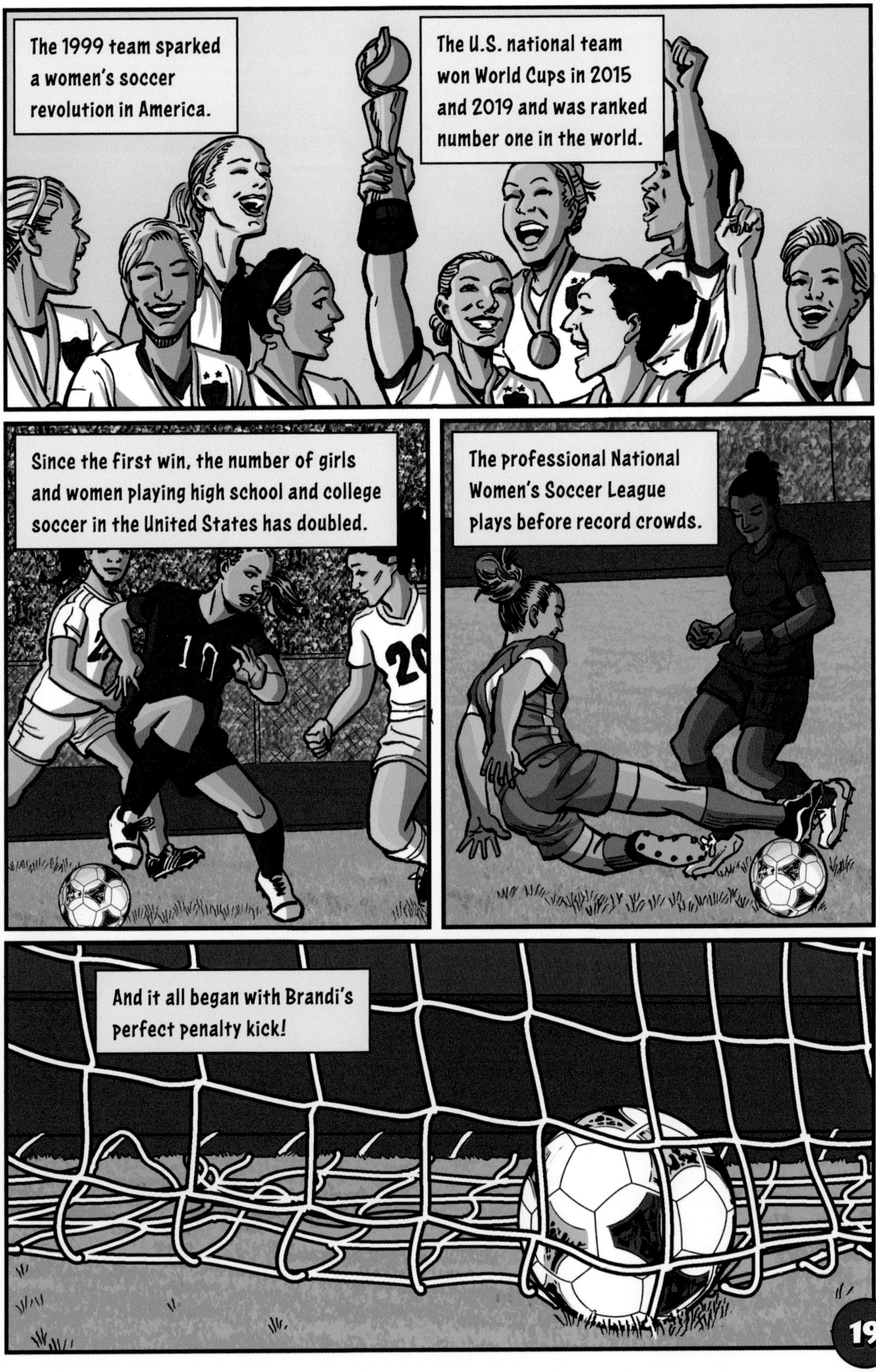
The 1999 team sparked a women's soccer revolution in America.
The U.S. national team won World Cups in 2015 and 2019 and was ranked number one in the world.
Since the first win, the number of girls and women playing high school and college soccer in the United States has doubled.
The professional National Women's Soccer League plays before record crowds.
And it all began with Brandi's perfect penalty kick!

WOMEN'S WORLD CUP

The Women's World Cup is held every four years. The tournament includes 32 of the world's best teams. They play against one another until the final two teams reach the championship game.

Since the first Women's World Cup in 1991, the event has grown in popularity and helped women's soccer around the world. The U.S. team often dominates the competition, having won the tournament four times. That is partly a result of the many opportunities for young girls growing up in the United States to play soccer.

However, in recent years, other countries have given America some competition. Women's pro leagues in Europe have become the best in the world. Pro men's clubs in South America started women's teams, and that has created more chances for young women from Colombia to Chile. In 2022, the Women's Africa Cup of Nations expanded from 8 teams to 12, while attracting record crowds to the games. The future of women's soccer looks bright.

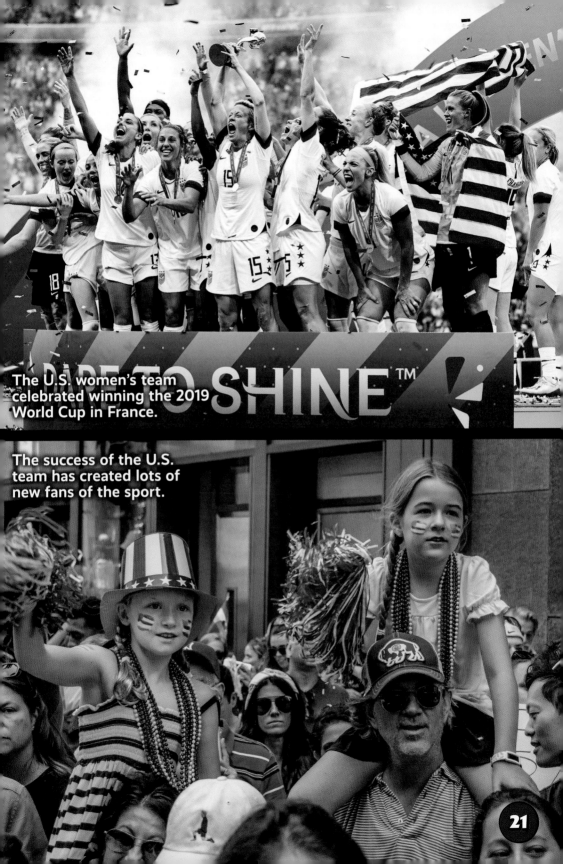

The U.S. women's team celebrated winning the 2019 World Cup in France.

The success of the U.S. team has created lots of new fans of the sport.

U.S. SOCCER STARS

Here are some of the best U.S. women's soccer players ever.

Mia Hamm scored 158 goals for the U.S. team while helping it win two World Cups and two Olympic gold medals. Born in Alabama, she played college and professional soccer throughout her career. After retiring, she helped form a new team in Los Angeles, California.

Abby Wambach has the second-highest number of wins of all professional female players around the world with 184 career goals for the national team. She helped the U.S. win the 2015 World Cup and two Olympic gold medals.

Megan Rapinoe was named the World Player of the Year in 2019 after she helped the United States win the World Cup. She has been a leader of the team both on and off the field.

Alex Morgan

Alex Morgan is another top goal-scorer for the U.S. She was co-captain of the 2019 World Cup champion team and also won gold and bronze medals in the Olympics.

GLOSSARY

defender in soccer, a position that plays near the goalie to help stop the other team from scoring

extra time in soccer, a period of play added to a game that ends in a tie

heads knocks the ball with the head

international between different countries

knock-out a type of playoff in which a team is out the first time they lose

penalty kick a free kick awarded for fouls inside the penalty box

professional someone who is paid money to play a sport

quarterfinal a playoff game when there are eight teams remaining

semifinal a playoff game when there are four teams remaining

tackle in soccer, knocking the ball away from an opponent by kicking or sliding

INDEX

READ MORE

Buckley, James Jr. *It's a Numbers Game: Soccer.* Washington, D.C.: National Geographic Kids, 2020.

Kelley, K. C. *Soccer: Score with STEM! (Sports STEM).* Minneapolis: Bearport Publishing Company, 2022.

Shaw, Gina. *What Is the Women's World Cup? (What Was?).* New York: Penguin Workshop, 2023.

LEARN MORE ONLINE

1. Go to **www.factsurfer.com** or scan the QR code below.
2. Enter **"Perfect Penalty Kick"** into the search box.
3. Click on the cover of this book to see a list of websites.